HOPES, NEEDS, RIGHTS & LAWS

How do governments and citizens manage
migration and settlement?

By Ceri Oeppen

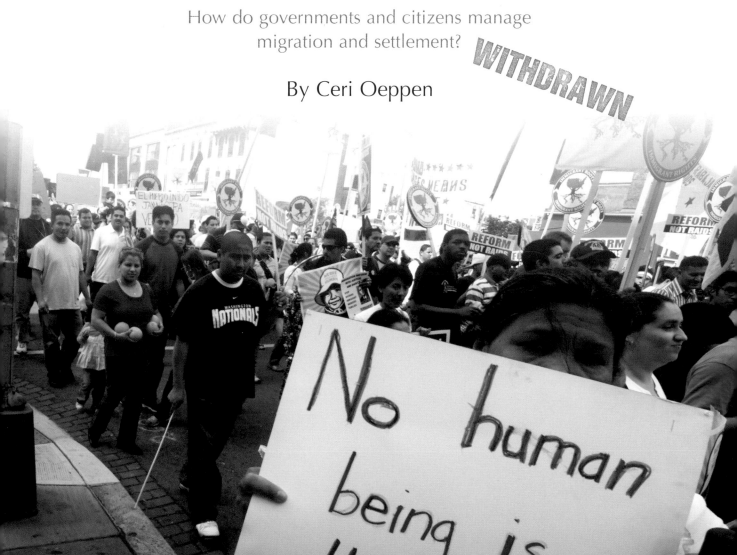

Crabtree Publishing Company

www.crabtreebooks.com

Author: Ceri Oeppen
Project director: Ruth Owen
Designer: Elaine Wilkinson
Editors: Mark Sachner, Lynn Peppas
Proofreader: Molly Aloian
Editorial director: Kathy Middleton
Prepress technician: Katherine Berti
Production coordinator: Margaret Amy Salter
Consultant: Dr. Julie Vullnetari, Sussex Centre
for Migration Research

Front cover (top): Immigrants and their supporters march to the White House, on International Workers' Day 2009, to call for legal reforms.
Front cover (bottom left): Refugees wait to cross the border from the Democratic Republic of Congo, in Africa, into Uganda in November 2008.
Front cover (bottom center): The Rainbow Bridge, over the Niagara River, between the United States and Canada.
Front cover (bottom right): A woman carries food distributed by the Red Cross at a refugee camp in Gori, Georgia.
Back cover: Survivors of the 2004 Indonesian tsunami living in a refugee camp in Aceh, Indonesia, in 2005.
Title page: In an attempt to stem irregular migration and punish employers who hire irregular migrants, U.S. government authorities may carry out workplace raids, showing up unannounced at workplaces and carrying out checks of workers' immigration documents. In this photo, immigrants and their supporters march to the White House to call for legal reforms and an end to such raids.

Photo credits:
Alamy: Joe Sohm: page 9; Bill Bachman: pages 18 (bottom), 19 (top); David Hoffman: page 38 (left); ArkReligion: page 39
Asylum Dialogues: Ben Kelly: pages 42–43 (bottom center)
Corbis: Charles Caratini: page 3 (left); David Brabyn: page 4 (center bottom); Christophe Calais: page 5 (bottom); Kevin Fleming: pages 6–7 (center); How Hwee Young: pages 12, 16 (top); Ed Kashi: pages 16–17 (bottom); Rick D'Elia: page 19 (bottom); Cathal McNaughton: pages 20–21 (bottom); Erich Schlegel: page 24 (bottom); Mona Reeder: page 28; page 30; Charles Caratini: pages 32, 34, 34–35; Andrew Holbrooke: page 36 (bottom); Peter Turnley: page 38 (bottom); Peter Dench: page 40
Getty Images: Melanie Stetson Freeman: page 8; Mufti Munir: page 13; Patrick Kovarick: pages 14–15 (top center); Jay Directo: page 23; Goh Chai Hin: page 29; page 31; Leon Neal: page 37
Ruby Tuesday Books Ltd: page 27
Shutterstock: front and back covers, pages 1, 3 (center left), 3 (center right), 4 (left), 5 (top), 6 (top), 7 (top), 10 (all), 14 (bottom), 18 (left), 20 (top), 22 (bottom), 24 (left), 25, 41, 42 (top), 43 (top all)
UNHCR, FIeld Information and Coordination Support Section, 2009: page 33
U.S. Department of State: Kay Chernush: pages 3 (right), 26 (top), 26 (bottom)
Wikipedia (public domain): pages 11, 22 (top)

Developed & Created for Crabtree Publishing Company by Ruby Tuesday Books Ltd

---

Library and Archives Canada Cataloguing in Publication

Oeppen, Ceri, 1980-
    Hopes, needs, rights & laws : how do governments and citizens manage migration and settlement? / Ceri Oeppen.

(Investigating human migration & settlement)
Includes index.
ISBN 978-0-7787-5180-9 (bound).--ISBN 978-0-7787-5195-3 (pbk.)

    1. Emigration and immigration--Juvenile literature.
2. Immigrants--Juvenile literature. I. Title.
II. Series: Investigating human migration & settlement

JV6201.O46 2010   j325   C2009-905266-0

Library of Congress Cataloging-in-Publication Data

Oeppen, Ceri, 1980-
  Hopes, needs, rights & laws : how do governments and citizens manage migration and settlement? / by Ceri Oeppen.
    p. cm. -- (Investigating human migration & settlement)
  Includes index.
  ISBN 978-0-7787-5195-3 (pbk. : alk. paper) -- ISBN 978-0-7787-5180-9 (reinforced library binding : alk. paper)
  1. Immigrants--Social conditions. 2. Immigrants--Services for. 3. Immigrants--Civil rights. 4. Illegal aliens. 5. Asylum, Right of. 6. Emigration and immigration--Social aspects. 7. Emigration and immigration--Government policy. I. Title. II. Series.

JV6225.O47 2010
325'.1--dc22
                               2009035003

Crabtree Publishing Company

www.crabtreebooks.com   1-800-387-7650

Printed in China/122009/CT20090915

Published in Canada
Crabtree Publishing
616 Welland Ave.
St. Catharines, ON
L2M 5V6

Published in the United States
Crabtree Publishing
PMB 59051
350 Fifth Avenue, 59th Floor
New York, New York 10118

Published in the United Kingdom
Crabtree Publishing
Maritime House
Basin Road North, Hove
BN41 1WR

Published in Australia
Crabtree Publishing
386 Mt. Alexander Rd.
Ascot Vale (Melbourne)
VIC 3032

CONTENTS

CHAPTER ONE

DIFFERENT TYPES OF MIGRANTS

People migrate for many different reasons. They also migrate for different lengths of time, or stay within the same country, or may cross an international border and become international migrants. International migrants may have permission to migrate, usually in the form of a document called a visa, or they may be migrating without permission and documents.

A Label for Every Migrant

Often, society and governments give migrants labels based on their reason for migrating, how far they migrate and for how long, and whether they have permission to migrate. For example, a person who "migrates" for two weeks to go sightseeing in a foreign country may be labeled an international tourist. Someone who migrates for two years to work in

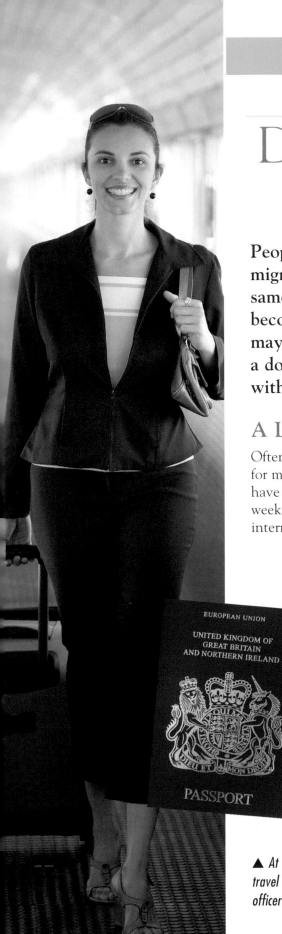

▲ At the U.S. border, foreign nationals must show their passport and a visa or other travel documents depending on their country of origin. A customs and border patrol officer will fingerprint travelers and take their photograph (seen here).

◀ Cars line up to cross the border between Canada and the United States. The border is the world's longest common border between two countries at 5,522 miles (8,886 kilometers) long.

another country may be labeled a temporary migrant worker. Other labels include economic migrant, irregular migrant, refugee, asylum seeker, and highly skilled migrant.

Reasons for Migrating

Some people migrate simply because they want new experiences and adventure. Most people migrate for political, economic, or family reasons, or for a combination of reasons. Often it is difficult to identify one single reason why a person migrates.

▼ During the Vietnam War (1959–1975) many of the Hmong people of Laos supported the United States against communist North Vietnam. When a communist movement took over Laos in 1975, many Hmong people fled to a refugee camp in Thailand. In the years that followed, Hmong refugees were allowed to settle in the United States. Here, Vang Xieng Yang arrives in Sacramento, California, to be greeted by relatives already living in the United States.

FOCUS ON:

THE QUESTION OF LABELS

For whatever reason people migrate from one country to another, immigration nearly always becomes a political issue that attracts strong feelings from people of all political beliefs. Debates about immigration can be fueled by labeling immigrants. These labels often place different types of immigrants into categories that are opposed to each other, such as *legal* vs. *illegal* immigrants, *forced* vs. *voluntary* immigrants, and *highly skilled* vs. *low-skilled* labor immigrants.

Any kind of labeling risks categorizing people very narrowly or inaccurately. Sometimes, these labels place people in categories that do not fairly represent their circumstances. For example, migrants from Lebanon, or another country with good educational institutions, might be highly educated and have a lot of professional work experience. They might be unable to find highly skilled employment in destination countries that do not recognize their educational qualifications. Immigrants in a situation like this may be forced into working at manual labor, which may inaccurately label them as low-skilled labor immigrants.

◄ *The term "alien" means outsider, or foreigner, and is sometimes used to describe immigrants. Some people think it is an unusual way to refer to people, because the term "alien" usually brings to mind beings from outer space! Here, a young Mexican American holds a sign with a cartoon picture of a space alien reading "we are human, not aliens."*

Some people may migrate voluntarily. For example, people may migrate to earn more money or to be closer to family. Others may be forced to migrate because of war or persecution. War and persecution are seen as political reasons for migration, and usually people who migrate for such reasons are labeled as refugees. Others may be forced to migrate because of drought or other environmental hazards.

Global Somalis

Since 1988, over one million people from the African nation of Somalia have been forced to migrate because of civil war. Some of these Somalis have moved within Somali, and hundreds of thousands have moved abroad to neighboring African countries, or to countries in the Middle East, Europe, and North America. It is often assumed that Somalis migrate for political reasons because of the war. The war has also damaged the economy and the related areas of education, health care, and other social services, and Somalis migrate for economic reasons, as well.

In addition to political and economic reasons for migrating, Somalis have a long history of nomadic migration that includes migrating to take livestock to new pastures. Somalis are renowned sailors who have been traveling across the world since the early 1800s. Considering their nomadic heritage, perhaps this helps to explain, in part, their mobility, and patterns of frequent migration today.

Migrating Where?

Internal migrants travel within the borders of one country. *International migrants* cross an international border and migrate to a foreign country. Sometimes, migrants are identified by the places to which they travel. For example, a farmer who goes to find work in the city might be called a rural-urban migrant. If a migrant travels back and forth between two or more places, this is called *circular migration*.

▶ *Many Somali people live a nomadic life, moving from place to place. Here, a woman assembles an aqal. This type of portable hut is dismantled and reassembled whenever the family moves.*

6

Another common type of migration, identified by destination, is called *return migration*. The majority of migrations are not permanent, and most migrants return to their place of origin. Return migration may be simply a visit, or it may be more long-term.

The Duration of Migration

Migrants are also classified by the length of time they spend as migrants. Two types are most common: temporary migrants (also known as sojourners) and permanent migrants. Migrants' ideas about how long they will stay in a new place may change over time and affect their classification as

▲ *An estimated 140 million Chinese people migrate within China each year. Most of these internal migrants are traveling east, from small towns and rural areas to the big cities where a boom in construction means there are large numbers of jobs.*

temporary migrants or as permanent migrants. Some migrants who intend to migrate permanently become homesick and decide to return, while some who intend to stay a short while decide to stay on.

Turkish Guest Workers in Germany

In the 1960s, many thousands of Turkish people, mostly men, traveled to what was then West Germany, under an agreement that allowed Turkish citizens to work on a temporary basis. From a German perspective, the aim of this program was to fill labor shortages. From a Turkish perspective, it was an opportunity for people to earn and save more money than they could in Turkey. The West German government soon lifted restrictions intended to stop Turkish migrants from staying too long. Although thousands of Turkish people returned to Turkey from West Germany, many more stayed on. In the 1970s, many brought over their wives and children to join them. People of Turkish descent are still the largest ethnic minority in Germany today.

▲ Somali immigrant Roda Abdullahi takes part in a class discussion during her English Language Learner (ELL) class at Como Park High School in St. Paul, Minnesota. Students immigrating to the St. Paul area are placed in the ELL program to help them learn and improve their English.

Migration and Citizenship

How do migrants stop being migrants? One way is to return to their country of origin. Another is to gain citizenship in their country of destination.

Some people believe that being a migrant is a "state of mind" and therefore can continue as an idea even after returning or gaining citizenship. Whatever the feelings a migrant may have about whether he or she will always be a "migrant" at heart regardless of nationality or citizenship, the governments of the world have their own ideas of what legally constitutes a migrant or a citizen.

The legal definition of a citizen varies from country to country. In most countries, being a citizen means being a "member" of the country and having the rights, privileges, and responsibilities that go with that membership. One right or privilege of citizenship may include being allowed to vote, while responsibilities may include paying taxes. In many countries, non-citizens such as permanent residents have similar rights and responsibilities.

Acquiring citizenship may also be easier in some countries than in others. Nearly every nation requires that migrants live there for a specified period of time. Many require that migrants have at least a basic ability to read and write the country's language and meet other criteria, such as not having committed any crimes in that country. Some nations require that applicants for citizenship give up their former citizenship, while others allow for dual or multi-citizenship—that is, citizenship in two or more countries.

JOURNEY STORIES

MR. FAHIM AND THE AMERICAN DREAM:

Mr. Fahim was born in Afghanistan. In the late 1970s, he worked for the Afghan government as a diplomat based in the United States. While he was in the United States, the Afghan government was overthrown and the Soviet Union invaded Afghanistan. It was unsafe for him to return to Afghanistan because he had worked for the previous government. So he stayed in the United States, even though his diplomatic position was taken away by the new Afghan government. Here is a brief description of the course his life took from that point:

We came to California in 1980 and found a cheap and good apartment. Then we found jobs, I worked with new refugees, supporting their resettlement. It was good, since my wife and I were both working, working hard, and we got our house and it was good ... What do you call it? "The American dream"—yes, you've got to have that dream in order to get somewhere here.

We really worked hard, working full-time and going to night school. After some time I applied for U.S. citizenship and I have been a citizen for over 20 years now. I would like to go back to Afghanistan some day, at least for a visit, but my children don't want to.

LAW OF THE SOIL AND LAW OF THE BLOOD

Citizenship laws are based on two contrasting ideas, which have Latin names: *jus solis* (law of the soil) and *jus sanguinis* (law of the blood). Countries that follow the principle of *jus solis* give automatic citizenship to people born within their territory. The United States, Canada, and the United Kingdom are examples. Countries that use the principle of *jus sanguinis* only give citizenship to people descended from citizens of that country. Until 2000, Germany used this approach. Now it also grants citizenship on a *jus solis* basis.

In practice, most countries' citizenship laws combine elements of both principles, even while favoring one over the other. Most countries also have the principle *jus domicile* (law of residence), whereby people who have lived legally in a country for a certain amount of time (for example, five years in the United States) can apply for citizenship.

◀ *A family from Tibet celebrates becoming U.S. citizens at a naturalization ceremony on Independence Day, July 4, 2005. The ceremony was held at Monticello, Thomas Jefferson's home in Charlottesville, Virginia.*

CHAPTER TWO

MANAGING ECONOMIC MIGRATION

Migration offers both challenges and opportunities to governments. On one hand, too many migrants may arrive and compete with local populations for jobs, housing, and natural resources. On the other hand, most governments recognize that migration is good for the economy. Migrants may fill gaps in the labor market by performing jobs that the local population is unwilling to do, such as cleaning or seasonal agricultural work.

◄ ▲ In the United States and United Kingdom, many agricultural jobs, such as fruit picking, are carried out by migrant workers (left). Workers from Mexico and other Latin American countries fill these roles in the United States, while workers from Eastern European countries often migrate temporarily to the United Kingdom to work on farms. In the United States, Canada, the United Kingdom, and New Zealand, over 25 percent of medical professionals are immigrants (above).

Finding One's Niche

At the other end of the scale, migrants may fill high-status positions because of their particular expertise in a "niche," or specialized, subject. A modern-day example of this kind of employment might be scientists hired to work in very specialized fields, such as space science or medical research.

The United States has a long history of encouraging migrants for specific projects. For example, Chinese and Irish laborers were brought in to build the Transcontinental Railroad in the 1800s. More recent examples come from the Cold War hostility between the United States and former Soviet Union. This period extended from the end of World War II in 1945 to the break-up of the Soviet Union and the end of other communist regimes throughout Eastern Europe in the early 1990s.

After World War II, weapons scientists from Germany and other countries in Central Europe were encouraged to bring their skills to the United States rather than the Soviet Union, which was then the United States' chief political, economic, and military rival.

Governments "manage" migration in order to limit the challenges and make the best use of the opportunities that migration brings. Governments try to do this in a number of ways: through the allocation of visas, the control of borders, and encouraging some types of migrants while discouraging others.

▲ Nazi Germany's premier rocket scientist, Wernher von Braun, was the architect of the V-2 rocket used to bomb London during World War II. After the war, he surrendered to the United States, where he used his talents to put astronauts into space. He is shown here with the U.S. Saturn V rocket that he designed — and that helped send men to the moon in 1969.

Selection in Managed Migration

One way that receiving countries manage immigration is by using visa regulations to make it easier for some people to migrate legally, while making it difficult, or even impossible, for others. In this way, governments can encourage migrants whose skills and attributes will contribute to what the government recognizes as the needs of its economy.

Many countries are interested in attracting skilled professionals, such as healthcare professionals and computing experts. Most countries have an immigration program for professionals who have been offered a job in that country.

MANAGING THE SPREAD OF INFECTIOUS DISEASES

Countries that have a long history of immigration such as the United States, Canada, and Australia assess immigrants' health as part of the immigration application process. In fact, the United States had rules requiring health checks of immigrants before more general immigration laws existed. Currently, immigrants to the United States have to show that they have been vaccinated against a list of infectious diseases, and immigrants can be refused a visa, or entry, on health grounds.

In countries with a shorter history of large-scale immigration, such as many European countries, health screening is not so established. For example, the United Kingdom only recently started screening visa applicants for tuberculosis, and only those from selected "sending" countries where there is a high recorded rate of tuberculosis. Most of those countries are in sub-Saharan Africa and South and Southeast Asia.

In these cases, the employer must provide proof of support for the applicant. This is usually called employer-sponsored immigration. Where this system exists, such as in the United States, immigrants must have a job offer before they apply for immigrant status.

Some countries such as Australia, Canada, and the United Kingdom have what are called "points-based" immigration programs, which allow highly skilled migrants to arrive without a job offer, on the understanding that they will apply for jobs after arriving. Under a points-based system, potential immigrants get points for things like higher education qualifications, income, work experience, and the relevance of their skills to the current skilled labor needs of the destination country. The more points they earn, the more likely they are to get a visa.

The U.S. Diversity Visa Lottery

Most immigration to the United States relies on potential immigrants having a sponsor, which means they have family already in the country or a job offer from a U.S. employer. The diversity visa lottery is a way in which people without these sponsoring families or employers can still immigrate to the United States.

The aim of the lottery is to encourage migrants from countries and regions that do not already contribute large numbers of immigrants to the United States. Migrants from countries from which more than 50,000 people have immigrated in the previous five years are ineligible. For example, in the 2010 program, applicants from Brazil, China, Colombia, the Dominican Republic, Ecuador, El Salvador, Guatemala, Haiti, India, Jamaica, Mexico, Pakistan, the Philippines, Peru, Poland, South Korea, the United Kingdom, and Vietnam were ineligible because more than 50,000 immigrants from each of these countries have migrated to the United States between 2005 and 2009.

◄ In 2009, a virus known as swine flu, which originated in Mexico, spread around the world. Some countries put health checks in place at their airports to try to stop the spread of the disease. Here, a health screening official at Changi Airport in Singapore checks the temperatures of passengers arriving in Singapore.

What About Low-skilled Migrants?

For potential immigrants who are not highly skilled, there are fewer options for legal migration. Those who have family in the destination country may be able to immigrate under a family reunification program. Family reunification allows immigrants to sponsor their relatives to join them. In the United States, green card holders are legal permanent residents who are not U.S. citizens but are allowed to live and work in the country for a designated length of time at a specific job. These residents can sponsor their children and spouse to join them. Those who are naturalized as citizens can also sponsor their parents, brothers, and sisters to join them.

For those who do not have relatives who can sponsor them, often their only chance is to apply for a temporary work permit. Governments of receiving countries usually have quotas of temporary work permits. Often, the employment sector is defined by the government in response to areas where there are shortages of low-skilled laborers. Employment sectors that commonly use migrant labor include seasonal agricultural work, hospitality and catering services, and domestic work such as cleaning or caring for the elderly.

Family reunification and temporary work permits are two ways in which low-skilled workers can migrate legally. A third way of migrating (for both highly skilled and low-skilled workers alike) is outside formal managed migration programs. This is called irregular migration, and it is discussed in chapter four.

▲ Anyone can apply for the diversity visa lottery in the United States, as long as they are from an eligible country and have a level of education that matches high school or above, or equivalent work experience and training. The lottery awards 50,000 visas per year. Here, thousands of hopefuls in Dhaka, Bangladesh, crowd into the General Post Office to submit their entries for the visa lottery.

THE TEN-POUND POMS

From 1947 through the 1950s and 1960s, more than 1.5 million British migrants traveled to Australia. Fewer than one-quarter of them returned to the United Kingdom, while the rest stayed permanently in Australia. Australians nicknamed them "ten-pound poms" because the Australian slang word for the English is "pom" and because they only paid ten pounds for the journey. At the time, the Australian government wanted to boost the white, non-Aboriginal population in Australia, so they subsidized the cost of the journey for people from the United Kingdom. This kind of program is called assisted migration.

Today, it is generally not acceptable to select migrants on the basis of race. Some argue, however, that the immigration programs of richer countries, such as Australia, the United States, and many European countries, which allow for permanent or long-term migration, focus too much on formal educational qualifications and work experience. So, even though people from sub-Saharan African countries and other less economically developed countries are not overtly racially discriminated against, the emphasis on formal education and work experience does put them at a disadvantage in gaining immigrant status.

Free Movement of Labor in the European Union

The free movement of European Union (EU) citizens for work and leisure purposes is part of the rights associated with being a member of the EU. In 2004 and 2007, the EU was enlarged to include countries in Eastern Europe. The citizens of these countries can now access labor markets in Western Europe, although with some temporary restrictions. EU citizens can migrate between EU countries without visas and without having to meet criteria on job sector or qualification level.

Controlling Borders to Manage Migration

In order to manage economic migration effectively, governments have to control the borders to their territory, allowing only those deemed eligible to enter as migrants. It is impossible to control the whole length of a border. Instead, governments use key points where migrants may enter the country, such as places where roads cross the border, sea and river ports, and airports as immigration checkpoints.

▲ U.S. border patrol agents are on constant alert for people trying to cross over into the United States secretly from Mexico as well as for smugglers trafficking in everything from illegal drugs to irregular migrants.

When a border intersects a major migration route, governments have to add extra border checks. Along the U.S.-Mexican border, immigration officials patrol to try to prevent migrants from crossing outside of official crossing points. In the Mediterranean Sea, immigration officials patrol by boat looking for migrants crossing from North Africa to southern Europe.

◀ *Thousands of migrants protest in Paris following the death of an irregular migrant who had jumped into a river to escape from the police. After World War II, the French government encouraged immigration, but since the early 1970s it has tried to restrict the number of migrants entering France.*

JOURNEY STORIES

CHRISTINIA:

Christinia is a migrant from Mexico living in Texas. Her family moved to the United States when she was four years old. At first, the family was on a temporary visa for 90 days.

We lived in a motel for about a month while my parents struggled to find a job. My mother found work first as a maid at a hotel that was a 20-mile [32-km] commute. (In the town) We found an old abandoned apartment that had no heat. We moved in there because it was only a 5-minute walk to my mother's job.

My father eventually found a job as a janitor. We had applied for permanent visas and after a long wait, we all had one. My mother and father got better paying jobs after a while and sent us to school, where we were constantly made fun of, but we still wanted to go so we could learn. We felt so privileged even though we didn't have much. We moved out of the apartment and into a better one, even though it took us a while to find one because no one wanted to sell an apartment to Mexicans. It has been a hard journey, but we made it.

► Security cameras at the airport in Portland, Maine, record terrorists Mohammed Atta (right) and Abdul Aziz Al-Omari as they board a flight to Boston. In Boston, the men would board American Airlines Flight 11, the plane that was flown into the North Tower of the World Trade Center.

The Impact of 9/11 on Immigration

The terrorist attacks of September 11, 2001, commonly referred to as 9/11, focused the attention of people and their governments on security. In particular, attention turned to how migration is managed and how governments check the identity and background of migrants. Although the terrorists involved in 9/11 were in the United States with visas, it appears that some had achieved this status through false documents.

After 9/11, controlling immigration and borders as a way of preventing terrorism became a key issue in debates and discussions about migration. Initially, the enhanced focus on security after 9/11 was targeted at migrants from Muslim countries, such as Iran, Syria, Iraq, and Pakistan, as well as at people who "looked" as if they might be Muslim. Some Muslims, even those who were naturalized citizens of non-Islamic countries, were discriminated against because of their religion and ethnic background. Over time, the focus on Muslim immigrants has been expanded to include most migrants. The United States has led the way in strengthening border security, with other countries following its lead.

The Migration Policy Institute, an organization in Washington, D.C., found that the impact of September 11 on temporary migration and refugee migration to the United States can be seen in immigration statistics. This is particularly the case in the steep fall in numbers of migrants from Pakistan, Bangladesh, Indonesia, and other Asian Islamic countries between 2001 and 2002. In these countries, migration dropped off by an average of 32 percent.

▼ *Americans of all backgrounds protest against random assaults on Muslims following the 9/11 terrorist attacks.*

USING THE U.S. PATRIOT ACT TO PREVENT TERRORISM

After September 11, 2001, the U.S. government passed the Patriot Act, which allowed intelligence officers to collect information on suspected terrorists, a group that may include immigrants and U.S. citizens. There has been debate in the United States, and globally, about how effective domestic intelligence gathering has been and whether it can prevent future attacks.

I personally believe that if these tools [in the Patriot Act] had been in law—and we have been trying to get them there for years—we would have caught those [9/11] terrorists. If these tools could help us now to track down the perpetrators—if they will help us in our continued pursuit of terrorists—then we should not hesitate to enact these measures into law. God willing, the legislation we pass today will enhance our abilities to protect and prevent the American people from ever again being violated as we were on September 11.

Orrin Hatch, Republican U.S. senator from Utah, speaking in Congress on October 25, 2001.

Muslims in America, about equally from South Asia, the Middle East and North Africa, and Southeast Asia, were targeted along with their institutions. The rationale for the U.S. government's action was that these people potentially support terrorism. Yet we now know, through the Report of the 9/11 Commission, that there were no domestic conspiracies of any significance at the time of the attacks, and there have been none revealed since. Of the more than 400 U.S. prosecutions of individuals on terrorism-related charges, virtually none charged were involved in a plot against America.

John Tirman, Executive Director of MIT's (Massachusetts Institute of Technology) Center for International Studies, writing on a Web site hosted by the Social Science Research Council, July 28, 2006.

▼ Even the simplest application form can become complicated if you do not speak the language in a new country where you have settled. Governments, local authorities, and other organizations often provide forms in a number of different languages to help newly arrived immigrants. Migrant community organizations also help new arrivals fill in forms.

THE NEEDS OF IMMIGRANTS

In many respects, the needs of immigrants are no different from those of a non-migrant. But because they are not citizens of the country in which they live, they do not have the same rights as citizens of that country. Even where immigrants do have rights, the government, employers, and society in general may put immigrants' needs below those of citizens.

What Sort of Needs?

As newcomers, immigrants may need support in becoming accustomed to a new culture and society. For example, they may need access to language classes or help finding places to live. They may need help finding work and getting information about their rights and responsibilities as residents of a new country.

Sometimes immigrants' particular needs might be related to the reason for their migration. For example, immigrants who arrive as refugees may need both physical and mental health support to help them deal with previous traumatic experiences. Migrants' needs may also be related to the manner in which they migrated. For example, those who were trafficked or otherwise underwent a difficult journey may also need extra health care or counseling.

▲ In Melbourne, Australia, the Department of Immigration provides an English language training program for adult migrants.

Who Helps Meet Immigrants' Needs?

Most of the day-to-day needs of migrants are met by family members and friends, especially those who migrated earlier. Often migrants' friends and family will give them somewhere to stay when they first arrive. They may also loan or give them money and help them find jobs. This is one reason that it is common to find certain economic sectors dominated by a particular migrant group. For example, in the United States by the late 1800s, many Chinese immigrants ran laundries, Italian immigrants ran ice cream carts, and Germans ran hot dog stands.

As well as help from family and friends, immigrants may also get help from the government of their destination country, charities, international organizations, religious institutions, or employers. The type of help immigrants get depends on their particular migration experience. Those who have come as refugees are more likely to get help from the social welfare department of the destination country's government, if such a department exists, as well as from charities, international organizations, and religious institutions. Highly skilled migrants or students often get relocation assistance from their employer or university.

▲ Italian immigrants sell Louis Granelli ice cream from a horsedrawn cart in England in the late 1800s.

▼ The Welcome to America Project supplies furniture, household goods, and help to refugees who have arrived in the United States with no possessions. Many have fled their home countries under difficult circumstances.

JOURNEY STORIES

ANNE:

When migrants first arrive in a country they often rely on friends and family to help them out. Employment is often found through information given by earlier migrants. Anne, a Korean immigrant, arrived in New York City in the mid-1970s and became established in the Korean "niche" business of working in, and operating, nail salons:

I would never have dreamed of becoming a nail salon owner myself... After graduating college I wanted to see what opportunities were in America. My older sister was living in New York City when I came. To earn money for graduate school, I looked for a job while staying with my sister. Through personal contacts, I got a job at the first nail salon in Queens. The owner was the Korean woman who pioneered this business in Manhattan... After three years of working there I started my own store... Employees from my first store, all Korean women, have become owners themselves.

United Nations Convention on Migrant Workers

The United Nations International Convention on the Protection of the Rights of All Migrant Workers and Members of their Families came into force as an international agreement in 2003. The aim of the Convention is to draw attention to the needs of migrant workers and protect their human rights. An important aspect of the Convention is that it recognizes that even migrants who entered a country illegally should have their human rights respected and be entitled to a basic level of assistance. Under the Convention, migrants who

▶ *Roma families carrying some of their possessions arrive at the Ozone Leisure Centre in East Belfast, Northern Ireland, on June 17, 2009. About 20 families, most of them migrants from Romania, had been forced to flee their homes and spend the night in a church hall following racist assaults on their homes. The attackers threw bricks through the windows of the families' homes in what police described as "hate crimes." The Roma, also known as Gypsies, have been targets of racial and ethnic discrimination across Europe for centuries.*

VIEWPOINTS

are residing in a country legally are entitled to an enhanced level of assistance, such as access to education and training for their family members.

Once a country has ratified, or accepted, the Convention, it is committed to respecting the duties and rights laid out in the Convention. It is interesting to note that so far, the countries that have ratified the Convention are those that send large numbers of migrants to other countries, including Mexico, the Philippines, and Egypt. It has not been signed by any countries that traditionally receive large numbers of migrants, including the United States, Canada, Australia, India, Saudi Arabia, or the United Kingdom and other countries in Western Europe.

Migration and Population Pressure

Migration is a "hot topic" in political discussions in many countries. One of the biggest concerns at the local level is the pressure that extra population may put on local services, such as housing, healthcare, education, and jobs. These concerns are made more pressing by the fact that migrants, particularly new migrants, often live in areas where there are already problems of poverty or overcrowding. In these areas, which attract some migrant groups because cheaper housing can be found there, local services are likely to already be overstretched. The perception that migrants may be getting any special treatment from local authorities can fuel resentment in other groups, as well as discrimination, racism, and xenophobia.

Migration and an Aging Population

In many richer countries, lower birth rates and higher life expectancies mean that the population is aging. In order to have a functioning economy and support the elderly, adding population through the arrival of migrants, especially young immigrants, may be essential.

MIGRATION AND PRESSURE ON LOCAL SERVICES

Many people living in areas that have high levels of immigration are concerned about the effect that migration has on local services such as housing, healthcare, and social welfare payments.

We found that public concerns about the effects of migration are not necessarily based on prejudice, but can arise from genuine anxieties about practical issues, such as the effect of migration on housing and other local services. The government needs to take action to respond to public concerns about the effects of migration. Local services are unable to respond to rapid population changes. [Also,] the government's funding allocations do not take into account the needs of local communities experiencing rapid inward migration. This situation is putting local public services under pressure.

Dr. Phyllis Starkey, Chair of the United Kingdom's Communities and Local Government Committee, 2008.

Those [migrant workers] who do come here make a huge contribution, particularly to our public services. Far from always or even mainly being a burden on our health or education systems, migrant workers are often the very people delivering those services. Now, a quarter of all health professionals are overseas born. Twenty-three percent of staff in our higher education institutions are non-UK nationals, and our public services would be close to collapse without their contribution.

Tony Blair (Prime Minister of the United Kingdom from 1997–2007), speaking to the Confederation of British Industries on April 27, 2004.

▲ *These vendors, most of them migrants from outside the European Union, set up "shop" on a street in Rome to hawk items on the black market. None of the euros (shown below) made on the items or paid to the workers will go directly to the government in the form of taxes.*

These young migrants will pay taxes and support the economy, which will in turn help fund the aging population's social security and retirement costs. Young migrants are also often the very people who look after the elderly, whether in institutions or live-in care. Care work is one of the most important sectors of employment for migrant women who come to work in industrialized aging societies in Europe and North America.

A Fair Deal for Migrant Workers' Taxes?

In most countries, workers pay taxes to the government as a percentage of the wages they earn. For countries with social security systems, such as the United States and Canada, some of these taxes are used to fund the social security payments that support people who are unable to work due to disability, illness, or old age.

Immigrants who decide to stay in their new country for the rest of their lives may see the benefits of the taxes they have paid, but what about temporary workers who pay taxes? Some countries have made agreements that pensions should be "portable," so that migrants who return to their homes can get the benefits their taxes have paid for. These agreements are mainly between rich countries and only affect fewer than 25 percent of migrants. Migrant workers from less economically developed countries who return to their country of origin have virtually no chance of seeing the long-term benefits of the taxes they paid.

According to a report by the Global Commission on International Migration, the lack of any return on the taxes they pay may encourage migrants to work in the "informal sector," or black market. In other words, they might work for employers who do not follow employment laws, particularly regarding taxation and insurance. These workers are more vulnerable to exploitation, such as lower pay for the work they do. They may also be discouraged from returning to their countries of origin.

The Need to Send Money Home

For many migrant workers, a key reason for migrating in the first place is to earn enough money that they can afford to send some of it home. This money, called remittances, is a hugely important source of income to families in migrant countries of origin. Countries where the amount of money sent is a large proportion of their domestic economy include Guyana, Tajikistan, Moldova, and Cape Verde. People living in other countries, such as Mexico, the Philippines, and India, receive larger incomes from remittances, but the domestic economies of those countries are larger to start off with, and families living there need more money. The World Bank estimates that migrants sent home $433 billion in remittances worldwide in 2008.

▲ Workers in the Philippines attend a job fair in Manila, the capital city of the Philippines, and sign up for job opportunities in the United States, Canada, Japan, and the Middle East.

TRES-POR-UNO PLAN

In some cases, remittances can be an important source of investment in development projects. The use of remittances for development has been recognized by many governments, in both migrant sending and receiving countries.

Mexican migrants send an estimated $24 billion a year back to Mexico. Most of this is sent to families, but some migrants send remittances to be invested in community development in the village or town they came from. In recognition of this input into the economy, the Mexican government introduced the *tres-por-uno* (three-for-one) plan in 2002. Under this plan, every dollar a migrant invests in a community project, such as building a church, highway, or health clinic, is matched by one dollar from the local government, one from the state government, and one from the federal government. So instead of the community project getting one dollar, it gets four.

CHAPTER FOUR

IRREGULAR MIGRATION

In chapter two we saw how the governments of "destination" countries manage migration by controlling their borders and by encouraging some types of migrants while discouraging others. In recent decades, the rules and regulations about immigration have become more restrictive. At the same time, the number of people wanting to migrate has increased.

Migrating Outside the Rules

Millions of people want to migrate, but are not eligible for visas under the migration management program of the countries they want to travel to. Perhaps they do not have the necessary qualifications and work experience, or they do not have family already there to sponsor their migration.

▲ It is not known how many people from Latin America die each year crossing deserts to reach the U.S. border, but officials estimate that about 400 Mexican migrants die annually due to dehydration, sunstroke, or hypothermia. Here, U.S. Customs and Border Protection officers round up a group of irregular immigrants trying to cross the U.S.-Mexican border.

▲ *In an attempt to stem irregular migration and punish employers who hire irregular migrants, U.S. government authorities may carry out workplace raids, showing up unannounced at workplaces and carrying out checks of workers' immigration documents. In this photo, immigrants and their supporters march to the White House to call for legal reforms and an end to such raids.*

As a consequence, some would-be migrants travel outside of formal migration regulations. They may avoid official border crossings so they are not questioned by immigration officials, or they may travel with counterfeit documents. Another option is to enter a country legally with a temporary visa but then stay on secretly after the visa ends or to enter a country and wrongfully claim asylum without due cause.

Irregular Migrants

The most widely accepted term for a person who migrates outside of formal channels is irregular migrant. The term "illegal immigrant" is often used by the media, but there are three reasons why people who advocate for migrant rights prefer not to use the word "illegal." First, this term dehumanizes migrants. A person cannot be "illegal," and migrants, whatever their status, are human beings with rights. Second, the term "illegal" wrongly links migrants with criminality. Most irregular migrants are not criminals, even though they have broken immigration rules. Third, for victims of persecution or violence whose lives are at risk, migrating outside of formal channels in order to get somewhere safe is more than just a convenient way of getting around the rules. It may be the only option available.

However necessary it might be for people to migrate outside of regular channels, doing so can be dangerous. In addition to exposing migrants to legal risks, irregular migration has the potential to bring migrants into contact with criminal elements, such as human trafficking networks.

Smuggling vs. Trafficking

Some irregular migrants escape immigration checks at borders by being transported by smugglers or human traffickers.

The words "smuggler" and "trafficker" are often used as if they mean exactly the same thing, but there are important distinctions between them.

Smuggled migrants voluntarily pay for the services of people to help them evade border controls or provide counterfeit travel documents. People involved in smuggling range from small networks of individuals whose aim is to help migrants to criminal gangs associated with organized crime. In the case of the latter group, the aim is to make a large profit from smuggling people across borders.

Trafficked migrants are transported against their will or lured into migration and exploitation through deception. For example, migrants might be recruited for jobs abroad and told that all their travel will be managed by middlemen. When they arrive, they may find that the "job" they have been promised turns out to be dangerous and exploitative, and they will not be given the opportunity to earn the money they were promised. Cases such as these often involve women working as servants in situations from which they cannot escape. Traffickers may take away their victim's passport or other documents, and she may be virtually trapped in her workplace, making her "employment" in effect a form of slavery.

▲ A desperate mother in Nepal holds a photograph of her teenage daughter who was trafficked into prostitution in Mumbai, India. Nepalese girls are lured by the traffickers with promises of a "good" job and the chance to improve their lives.

▼ These workers from Burma look to the commercial fishing industry in Thailand as a way to a better life. Many workers are trafficked onto ships and then kept at sea for months or even years. If they ask to be put ashore, they risk being fired and not paid for their work.

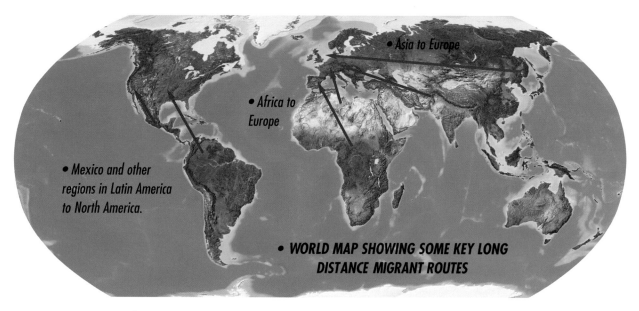

- Asia to Europe
- Africa to Europe
- Mexico and other regions in Latin America to North America.

• **WORLD MAP SHOWING SOME KEY LONG DISTANCE MIGRANT ROUTES**

Dangerous and Expensive Journeys

In order to avoid being caught by immigration authorities, irregular migrants undertake long, difficult, and dangerous journeys. Few migrants can afford false documents and airplane tickets. Instead, they travel on foot, in small boats, under trains, or in the back of trucks. Many irregular migrants put their lives at risk to get to their destination.

Traveling from Southern Africa to Europe involves crossing the Sahara Desert, followed by a dangerous journey across the Mediterranean Sea in small boats that are usually overcrowded and not suited to such a long journey. It is estimated that 2,000 migrants die per year trying to cross the Mediterranean. Traveling from Asia to Europe usually involves hiding in trucks, and migrants have been found dead from suffocation and dehydration. Traveling across the U.S.-Mexican border can also mean crossing inhospitable environments, including the Sonoran and Chihuahuan deserts, both of which straddle the U.S.-Mexican border.

JOURNEY STORIES

MORGAN:

Morgan is a 30-year-old Nigerian who has tried to reach the Canary Islands (which belong to Spain) by crossing the Sahara Desert and then sailing out to sea:

I tried to get to the Canary Islands once before but didn't make it, I'm on my way back to try a second time. The boat I was on was intercepted by the Spanish police as we reached land. I was deported back to Nigeria. That journey [on the smugglers boat] was quite possibly the most frightening experience of my life and had we not been picked up by the authorities, we would all have died. Despite this, I am on my way back, to try again.

Life in Nigeria is hard. There is such poverty. There are no jobs, there's no food and there is corruption. I can't say too much, as I fear for the lives of my family left behind.

I have to try and make a better life for myself and send money back for my family.

MIGRANT AMNESTIES

Given the risks associated with irregular migration—as well as the loss of taxes through people working in the informal economy and a feeling that governments should know who has migrated to their country—some people think that all irregular migrants should become fully documented, or "regularized." One way of accomplishing this would be for the government to declare an amnesty. Such a program would allow irregular migrants to come forward and be given documents that give them a legal status in the country in which they reside. Some people, however, think that this will encourage more irregular migrants to arrive in the hope that after some time there will be another amnesty. Some countries, such as Italy and Spain, have used amnesties, and other countries, including the United States and United Kingdom, are considering them.

Legalizing undocumented workers would improve wages and working conditions for all workers, and increase tax revenues. Moreover, comprehensive immigration reform that includes a path to legalization for undocumented workers should pay for itself through the increased tax revenue it generates, in contrast to the failed and costly enforcement-only policies that have been pursued thus far. Newly legalized workers [would also] spend more on goods and services.

The Immigration Policy Center, Washington D.C.

Adoption of an amnesty would increase the number of persons eligible for social assistance. Moreover, granting amnesty to illegal aliens would send the message around the globe that the United States no longer believes in the rule of law and is not willing to punish those who violate it.

The Federation for American Immigration Reform, Washington D.C.

▲ Crime scene workers examine a truck in which people from Mexico were trying to cross into the United States. The back of the truck was unventilated and 18 of the migrants died.

As well as being dangerous, such journeys are expensive. In 2008, for example, some Afghans were paying $16,000 each to be smuggled into the United Kingdom. Many migrants borrow the money with the intention of paying their lenders back when they arrive and find work. If they get caught en route or are deported before they have time to pay back the money, they will have huge difficulties ever paying their lenders, and they and their families may be threatened or harassed by those who advanced them the money.

Exploitation of Migrants Without Formal Status

Irregular migrants are likely to be exploited by unscrupulous employers who see them as a cheap and expendable source of labor. They are usually paid below a minimum wage and then have to work above maximum hours to earn enough money to survive and send money to their families. They cannot complain about exploitation or poor treatment to the police or local government because they are afraid of being caught.

Often, irregular migrants are also too afraid of deportation to risk accessing health care. This may contribute to the spread of infectious diseases as well as threaten the migrant's own health.

Although many irregular migrants are paid in cash, it is estimated that many pay taxes. In the United States, for example, an estimated half of irregular migrants pay taxes. For these people, it seems especially unfair that they cannot access health care and other public services.

▼ *Yu Lihong visits the grave of her husband with her mother-in-law Shi Aizhu. Yu's husband, Guo Binglong, was one of the cockle pickers who died at Morecambe Bay in the United Kingdom. The family live in the tiny fishing village of Zelang in the southeast of China. Like many Chinese migrants, Guo Binglong left his home and traveled thousands of miles in the hope of earning money to send back to his family.*

FOCUS ON:

MORECAMBE BAY COCKLE PICKERS

In early 2004, 23 Chinese irregular migrants were killed while collecting cockles from the sands of Morecambe Bay in the United Kingdom. The agent who had employed them had apparently sent them out on the sand at the wrong time of day, and they were stranded and drowned as the tide came in.

The tragedy caused the UK government to introduce the Gangmasters Licensing Act 2004, which aims to regulate the employment agencies, or middlemen, who employ migrant labor in agricultural and fishing work.

Meanwhile, according to an investigation by the *Guardian* newspaper in London, the families of the migrants who died at Morecambe Bay still struggle to repay the money they had borrowed to pay for their migration.

In 2006, the story of the Morecambe Bay cockle pickers was made into a documentary film called *Ghosts*, directed by Nick Broomfield.

CHAPTER FIVE

REFUGEES & ASYLUM SEEKERS

The terms "refugee" and "asylum seeker" are often used as if they mean the same thing, but they actually have distinct meanings. Asylum seekers have left their country of origin to claim protection from another country or the international community and are seeking asylum, or a place of safety. Refugees are people whose need for protection has been recognized. They have sought asylum, their claim of being persecuted has been recognized, and they have been given refugee status under international law.

◀ ▲ *December 1945—World War II has ended, and starving, homeless, and stateless Polish Jews in Berlin, Germany, gather around a cart that is bringing them their daily ration of one loaf of bread for each four persons. Around 5,000 Jews from Poland came to Berlin to find out where they would be sent next. Many hoped it would be Palestine or the United States.*

▲ When India became the Hindu nation of India and the Muslim nation of Pakistan after gaining independence from British rule in 1947, millions of people became refugees as they tried to migrate to the nation where they felt most secure. Around 10 million Hindus migrated from Pakistan into India, while 7.5 million Muslims migrated from India to Pakistan. Here, Muslim migrants are waiting to move into Pakistan at the Puran Qila refugee camp in Delhi, India.

The 1951 Convention: Who Is a Refugee?

After World War II, there were large numbers of refugees in Europe but no single organization to support them or regulations to give guidance on their protection. In response, the United Nations High Commissioner for Refugees (UNHCR) was formed at the beginning of the 1950s. In 1951, the UN Refugee Convention was introduced. That set of standards, including some changes made in 1967, defines a refugee as follows:

[Any person who,] owing to well-founded fear of being persecuted for reasons of race, religion, nationality, membership of a particular social group or political opinion, is outside the country of his* nationality and is unable or, owing to such fear, is unwilling to avail himself of the protection of that country; or who, not having a nationality and being outside the country of his former habitual residence, is unable or, owing to such fear, is unwilling to return to it.

[*Although the Convention uses the terms "his" and "himself," this is a reflection of the era in which it was written, and the Convention definition applies to both men and women.]

REFUGEES IN EUROPE AFTER WORLD WAR II

The United Nations High Commissioner for Refugees (UNHCR) estimates that at the end of World War II, an estimated 40 million people were displaced, without homes, in Europe.

These 40 million people came from all sides of the conflict. Most people are aware of the tens of millions of people who had been transported to concentration camps by Nazi Germany as prisoners, laborers, or targets of the Nazis' efforts to exterminate Jews and other minorities throughout Europe. At the end of the war in Europe, these people were freed by the Allied forces, but the majority of them had no home to go to. There were also tens of millions of Germans who had been expelled from the Soviet Union and Eastern European countries such as Poland and Czechoslovakia. At the same time, over one million people were fleeing from repression in the Soviet Union. In addition, civil conflicts in southeastern Europe also caused the displacement of Greeks and others following World War II.

This was the context that led to the establishment of the Refugee Convention in 1951.

Regional definitions also exist in Africa and Latin America, but the UN Refugee Convention definition remains the most significant statement on who is a refugee. Over 141 countries have signed up to respect the Convention, which means they must recognize that people who fit the Convention definition are refugees, with a right to protection.

The Principle of Non-Refoulement

One of the most important principles of the Refugee Convention is the principle of *non-refoulement*, which means that refugees cannot be forcibly returned to the situation they fled. This principle also applies to people whose refugee status has not yet been confirmed or is in the process of being decided upon—in other words, asylum seekers. Because of the principle of *non-refoulement*, governments have a duty to at least consider people's claims for asylum. When governments do not do this, such as the alleged case of the African nation of Tanzania closing its border to those fleeing genocide in Rwanda in 1994, they are said to be violating the principle of *non-refoulement*.

Large-Scale Refugee Emergencies— How Do Governments Cope?

The protection needs of refugees are potentially large and complex. Many refugees flee their country of origin in a hurry and arrive in a new country with no money, shelter, or food. As the victims of persecution, or the fear of persecution, they may also need psychiatric services related to their traumatic experiences. If they have fled conflict and violence, or traveled in difficult circumstances, they may also need medical attention.

Refugee emergencies are often made up of large groups of people traveling at the same time. Consequently, it can be a logistical challenge to make sure that everyone is provided with shelter, food, clean water, sanitation, and medical services.

These challenges may be compounded by the fact that the largest refugee populations are almost all under the protection of less economically developed countries, as the following numbers show. The figures also show how important Africa is as both a source and a destination of refugees. In order to cope with these refugee populations, most governments have to rely on the assistance of the international community, especially UNHCR.

▲ In 1994, political upheaval in the central African nation of Rwanda led to the murder of over 700,000 ethnic Tutsis and their sympathizers by Hutus. At the same time, another two million refugees from both groups streamed across the borders separating Rwanda from its neighbors, principally Tanzania and Uganda, placing huge strains on those nations' resources, utilities, and other services.

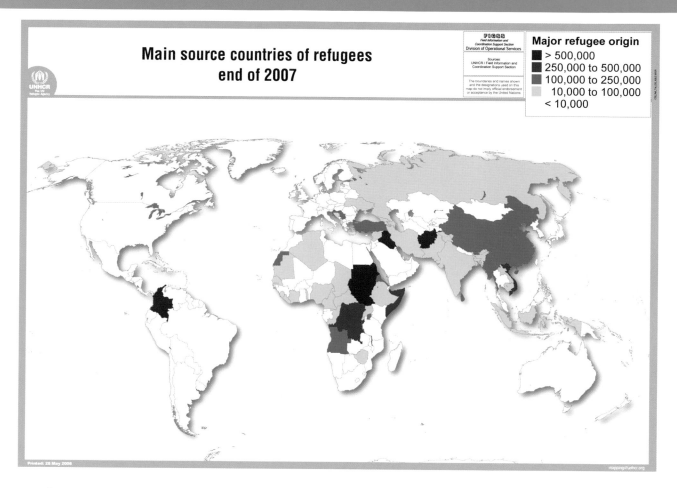

The government of the receiving country usually provides the land for the refugee camp or settlement, while UNHCR manages the emergency assistance to the refugees. UNHCR works with other UN agencies such as the World Food Program and the World Health Organization to provide food and health care for refugees. UNHCR also works with international and local Non-Governmental Organizations (NGOs) to provide other assistance to refugees, such as shelter materials, water, and sanitation.

Top six refugee countries of origin and key countries of asylum		
Country of origin	**Number of refugees**	**Top two countries of asylum**
Afghanistan	2.8 million	Pakistan, Iran
Iraq	1.9 million	Syria, Jordan
Somalia	0.6 million	Kenya, Yemen
Sudan	0.4 million	Chad, Uganda
Colombia	0.4 million	United States of America, Ecuador
Democratic Republic of Congo	0.4 million	Congo, Rwanda

Data: from UNHCR, 2007.

▲ Afghan children attend an open-air class at a refugee camp on the outskirts of Pakistan's capital, Islamabad. The education of girls was banned under Taliban rule in Afghanistan, and many girls at the refugee camp are attending lessons for the first time in their lives.

The Afghan Refugee Crisis

Since the Soviet invasion of Afghanistan in the late 1970s, and with subsequent events in that country, including the U.S.-led invasion following the attacks of 9/11, Afghan refugees have been the largest refugee population to which UNHCR has provided assistance. In the early 1990s, the Afghan refugee population peaked at around 6.2 million. Although it has dropped since then, it is still almost one million larger than the next-biggest UNHCR-assisted group, Iraqi refugees.

Over time, Afghan refugees have migrated all over the world, but over 90 percent remain in Pakistan and Iran alone. These two nations have reacted quite differently to the arrival of Afghan refugees. Nevertheless, the governments of both countries have seen the protection of Afghan refugees as part of their Islamic duty, at least during the first ten years of conflict in Afghanistan, when it was occupied by the Soviet Union between 1979 and 1989.

Pakistan settled most of its Afghan refugees in refugee camps and asked for the assistance of UNHCR and other international organizations. In contrast, Iran allowed Afghans to settle in urban areas and supported the Afghan refugees

for many years with very little outside support. Some suggest this is because Iran suspected the United Nations, and UNHCR, as being a tool used by Western governments, particularly the U.S. government, to gain influence and power over other countries.

Forced Migrations—Many Categories

Some people argue that the 1951 Refugee Convention definition of who is a refugee is too narrow. Many people point out that people may be forced to migrate for other reasons than persecution or fear of persecution. People may be forced to migrate due to war, poverty, environmental hazards, and development projects such as large dams.

In 1969 the Organization of African Unity (OAU) adopted an additional definition of who is a refugee to include people who were compelled to flee to another country due to "external aggression, occupation, foreign domination or events seriously disturbing public order." The members of the OAU felt that this definition more accurately represented people in "refugee-like" situations in Africa.

Some organizations have tried to get the category "environmental refugee" recognized to define people who have been forced to flee due to environmental hazards or climate change. For example, the category "environmental refugee" would include the hundreds of thousands of people who were forced to flee their homes due to damage caused by the Indian Ocean tsunami in 2004. This change has been resisted by many who feel that the addition of the category "environmental refugee" will push the already inadequate resources for refugee protection too far and "dilute" the significance of the 1951 Refugee Convention.

◄ Following the birth of Israel in 1948, Arab states in the region declared war on the new Jewish state. Some Arabs stayed in what would become Israel, but many left (as seen in this photograph from June 1948), fearing for their safety in what had become a Jewish nation. Today's Palestinian refugees are those people who lost their homes as a result of that conflict, plus their descendants.

PALESTINIAN REFUGEES

One refugee population is even larger than the Afghan one: Palestinian refugees. They are not recorded in UNHCR statistics because there is a special UN agency to support them called the United Nations Relief and Works Agency for Palestine Refugees in the Near East (UNRWA). UNRWA has 4.6 million Palestinian refugees registered as eligible for protection.

The plight of Palestinians today has a complex history. This history includes Britain's takeover of the ancient region of Palestine earlier in the 1900s, the movement for a national homeland for Jews after the murder of millions of European Jews by Nazi Germany during World War II, and the establishment of that homeland in Palestine, as the State of Israel in 1948. At the time, the plan was to divide, or partition, Palestine into two states, one Arab and one Jewish. Millions of Arab Palestinians found themselves in the middle of a plan—and a resulting Arab-Israeli conflict—that they had no control over.

Internally Displaced Persons (IDPs)

Another feature of the 1951 Refugee Convention, and the OAU definition, is that they only include migrants who have fled from their country of origin and crossed an international border into another country.

As previous chapters have shown, international migration is subject to many restrictions, and if migrants travel outside of formal channels, it can be extremely expensive. These restrictions prevent many people in "refugee-like" situations from fleeing their country of origin entirely. Those who are able to leave only the village, town, or region they come from are known as internally displaced persons (IDPs).

There are an estimated 26 million IDPs globally, which is a larger population than that of the state of Texas. Often, countries that are the source of large international refugee populations also have large IDP populations. According to the Internal Displacement Monitoring Centre, most of the top six refugee countries of origin have even larger numbers of IDPs: Sudan, 4.9 million; Colombia, 2.6-4.3 million; Iraq, 2.8 million; the Democratic Republic of Congo, 2 million; Somalia, 1.3 million; and Afghanistan, 0.2 million. The vast majority of IDPs are living in poor countries, and only some of them can be reached by organizations like UNHCR to be given assistance.

◀ In 2004, an undersea earthquake off of Sumatra, Indonesia, triggered a tsunami, or tidal wave, that devastated coastal regions of many nations on the Indian Ocean. The tsunami killed an estimated 230,000 people. It also left over 1.5 million homeless, including this woman, shown in a camp for internally displaced persons (IDPs) in Sri Lanka.

IDPs in Pakistan

The fundamentalist Islamist group known as the Taliban has been operating an insurgency, or rebellion, against the governments of Afghanistan and Pakistan since its removal from power in Afghanistan by U.S.-led forces in 2001. Since 2008, Pakistan has been fighting the Taliban in the northwest of Pakistan, in areas near the border with Afghanistan. Hundreds of thousands, even millions, of people have been forced to flee their homes because of fighting between insurgents and government forces.

The Pakistani government has established camps for these displaced people, but many have complained of lack of food, water, medicines, and blankets. The fighting in the area has limited the amount of help brought to IDPs by the International Committee of the Red Cross and other international humanitarian organizations. In addition to the ongoing fighting, both sides of the conflict—the Taliban militants and the Pakistan army—have made it difficult for international organizations to get access to the camps to help those living there.

◀ Men fill water drums from an underground water main in Monrovia, the capital of Liberia, in April 2008. Land disputes and continued political and ethnic tensions have hampered efforts to bring back all of the refugees and IDPs who fled their homes during the time of war.

JOURNEY STORIES

PAUL:

Between 1989 and 2003, citizens of the African nation of Liberia suffered through a long and deadly civil war. The UNHCR estimates that over 75,000 Liberian refugees remain outside of their country, the majority in the nearby countries of Côte d'Ivoire, Ghana, Guinea, Nigeria, and Sierra Leone. Paul had to leave Liberia because of fighting between government and rebel soldiers. He escaped to the neighboring country of Sierra Leone, but he does not know if the rest of his family is alive.

I hope they are alive and doing fine somewhere in Liberia. I am happy to be in Freetown where I do not hear any gunshots. When I fled Liberia, I had no time to pack my books and other learning materials to take with me. I don't go to school now. I cannot afford to go. If I could go back to school, I would like to study to become a nurse. I would like to go to school because it means I can become self-reliant and hold a responsible position in society. I feel I am an idler here because I am not going to school. I am not doing anything that will help me earn a decent future. I will go back [to Liberia] immediately if there is peace and security in my country.

CHAPTER SIX
PROMOTING TOLERANCE

Previous chapters have looked at the way in which governments and other institutions can manage migration and support the needs of migrants, particularly forced migrants such as refugees. Governments and social institutions, as well as society more generally, can also play a role in supporting migrants by promoting the tolerance of social and cultural differences.

When Intolerance Prevails

The failure of migrants and local populations to tolerate each other's differences can lead to misunderstandings, outbreaks of racism, and, in extreme cases, civil unrest. In the summer of 2001, for example, in

▲ A young man watches as businesses burn following the 1992 Los Angeles riots. The riots occurred after a widely publicized case of police brutality. In that racially charged case, a jury with no African Americans on it acquitted several white Los Angeles police officers in the videotaped beating of African-American motorist Rodney King.

◄ Members of a racist political party, the National Front, take part in a demonstration against Islam in London, 2007.

38

◀ *Children from different cultures in London take part in a play as part of their school's celebration of Diwali, the Hindu festival of lights.*

STRUCTURAL INTEGRATION AND SOCIO-CULTURAL INTEGRATION

The integration of immigrants into a larger culture can be divided into two main types: structural integration and socio-cultural integration. Structural integration refers to practical changes that immigrants and societies make to help migrants become included in the day-to-day and economic life of their new country. Examples of structural integration include having a bank account, gaining stable employment, renting or buying an apartment or house, voting, and gaining citizenship.

Socio-cultural integration refers to changes in outlook, social life, and cultural practices. Examples of socio-cultural integration may include language learning, making new friends, listening to new music, watching new television programs, or joining new clubs or associations.

Bradford, United Kingdom, riots broke out after ongoing tensions reached a boiling point between Asian youth and two anti-immigration political parties, the British National Party (BNP) and the National Front (NF). An earlier example of civil unrest fueled by racial tensions is the Los Angeles riots in 1992, where more than 50 people were killed and thousands were injured or arrested. The Los Angeles riots were caused, in part, by what many people felt was the unfair treatment of African Americans by the police and judicial system.

Encouraging Cultural Integration

Cultural integration is the process by which migrants and the local population, or members of mainstream culture, gradually adapt to each other. People alter their activities and opinions so they can live and work comfortably alongside each other.

Cultural integration affects both migrants and the mainstream. For integration to be successful, both sides need to adapt. As migrants are usually the minority population, they are more likely the ones who make the larger adaptations in their lifestyles.

Cultural integration is also a process of gradual adaptations and accommodations. It does not necessarily mean that migrants and the local population become culturally identical. While integration may happen over time, particularly in areas such as language, employment, and education, it may be less likely to occur in areas where beliefs and practices are more firmly rooted or strongly felt, such as religion. Even though there may be areas where cultural integration is less likely to occur, the eventual aim should be for equality of opportunity and equal rights and responsibilities among migrant and non-migrant groups alike.

A Case in Point—South Asians in California

Based on U.S. census data, California's large immigrant population from South Asia, particularly India, has the same, and sometimes higher, levels of income, educational qualifications, and employment status as does the mainstream U.S. population. The opportunities available to Indian immigrants and their children are, in many ways, equal to those of other Americans in California. In this way, Indian immigrants can be seen as successfully integrated, even though they may have different religious beliefs, eat different foods, or speak a different language at home than other Americans.

People who believe in promoting tolerance suggest that governments, non-governmental organizations such as community or religious institutions, and individuals, should encourage integration by accepting and celebrating differences even while encouraging activities that help promote equality between migrants and non-migrants.

◄ *Friends at Villier's High School, Southall, West London, enjoy a joke during a break from classes. There are 57 nationalities at the school speaking 51 different languages and representing 18 different religious sects.*

▼ *Through the Time Together organization's TimeBank program, refugees get individual help adapting to a new country. Mentors get to learn about other cultures and traditions. Hopefully, they both get to make a new friend!*

Going to Language Classes ... with My Mom and Dad!

A key component of integration is the ability for migrants and non-migrants to communicate with each other. Governments and communities should try to provide appropriate language-learning opportunities for migrants and recognize that many migrants work long hours and may not be able to spend a lot of time studying.

For migrant parents, learning the language of their new country will help them become more involved in their children's school activities, which can help their children get better grades.

In the city of Frankfurt, Germany, schools have introduced language classes that parents are encouraged to attend. The language classes focus on practical German, for day-to-day life. In addition to offering language lessons, these classes provide an opportunity for migrant parents to meet other parents in a similar situation. The parents also get to meet their children's teachers and learn more about the school system in Germany because their classes are held at their children's schools. This helps parents help their children.

Time Together—a Mentoring Program for Refugees

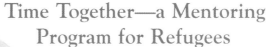

While the government and other institutions may be able to encourage integration through various programs and informative publications, probably the best way to adapt to a new country and learn how it works is to make friends with someone who grew up there. Meeting and making friends can be very difficult for migrants, especially for adult migrants who cannot make friends at school.

In London and Glasgow, in the United Kingdom, the organization TimeBank has set up a program called Time Together. Time Together matches individual refugees with a mentor, someone who has been in the country for a long while or who grew up there. The mentor and refugee are matched with each other on the basis of their interests.

Mentors can help their refugee partners with practical issues such as how to use public transportation and apply for jobs. A mentor can also just be a friend to meet for a coffee and a chat, and to share experiences and stories with.

◀ *The annual Irish feast day of St. Patrick's Day is celebrated by Irish immigrants and many other revelers in countries around the world. When cultural celebrations and events are supported by local authorities, they can help people feel that their celebrations are respected by the government and people of their new country. Here, an Irish marching band takes part in a parade in Boston.*

Celebrating Diversity

Promoting tolerance is about more than simply helping migrants adapt to their new country. It is also about encouraging both migrants and non-migrants to celebrate diversity and difference and to respect each other's cultures.

In multicultural countries like the United States, Canada, and the United Kingdom, particularly in big cities, it is common to see positive displays of cultural differences in celebrations and other community events such as Chinese New Year, Mardi Gras, Diwali, and St. Patrick's Day. Celebrating these events can be a good opportunity for people of different cultures to learn about each other.

Another aspect of cultural difference that is frequently "celebrated" is food. People from all different cultural and ethnic backgrounds regularly consume food that comes from a different cultural heritage than their own.

Going to the Library

New York City is one of the most culturally diverse cities in the world, and its borough of Queens is itself home to a wide variety of cultures. The more than 60 library branches in the Queens Library system act as centers for community activities for both migrants and non-migrants. Since the 1970s, Queens Library has provided language classes and information seminars for newcomers. Its "New Americans Program" organizes events to help immigrants adapt to their new homes. These events include talks on how to set up a business or how to apply for citizenship. The program also holds events to celebrate different cultural festivals.

In addition to supporting integration through educational programs and events, the library also responds to the entertainment and information needs of its diverse group of readers. The library provides newspapers and books in a variety of languages.

Governments do their best to manage immigration through visas, border control, and the granting of refugee status. In addition to enforcing the rules and restrictions of their immigration policy, most governments also try these methods to help immigrants make the most of the opportunities immigration offers, while trying to limit the challenges that arise.

▶ *Italian, Indian, Chinese, Mexican: These are all popular cuisines in many countries of the world, not just Italy, India, China, and Mexico. Often, these cuisines are adapted to suit local tastes, which results in a fusion of flavors and tastes. Here, from top left clockwise: Indian samosas, Chinese dim sum, Italian ravioli, and Mexican enchilladas with guacomole.*

For immigration to be positive for all concerned, including the migrants and the communities where they live, people need to get to know each other and respect each other's differences. It is often easier to learn about other people through personal connections and interactions. This is why small-scale projects such as those at Queens Library, or the Time Together program, all of which bring people together in a supportive environment, are a good way of "managing" what happens after an immigrant arrives.

◀ *In the United Kingdom, a theater company has tried to improve understanding about asylum seekers' experiences through the production Asylum Dialogues.*

GLOSSARY

amnesty A time period when people may admit to certain wrongdoings, such as migrating without a visa, without getting into trouble

asylum Protection given to people who have left their country because of persecution

black market Buying and selling of products or services, against or outside of formal laws and regulations

census An official survey that counts the number of people living in a country, as well as other information about them such as age, gender, and occupation

deportation Officially removing someone from a country, for example, forcing an irregular migrant to leave

destination country Any country to which migrants travel

drought A shortage of rain, or water more generally, that leads to the drying out of soil and the failure of crops

ethnic Belonging or relating to a particular group of people, identified on the basis of their racial, national, or cultural background

fundamentalist Strictly adhering to the traditional teachings of a religion

fusion The mixing, or melting together, of different things

green card A card that identifies the holder as a non-U.S. citizen who has permission to live and work permanently in the United States

hospitality Relating to businesses in which people are provided food, housing, and entertainment, such as restaurants, hotels, and bars

indigenous Native to or originating from a particular place, usually at or near where it is found

logistical Having to do with coordinating many people, organizations, and supplies

lottery A competition where the winners are picked randomly from all those who enter

mentor Someone who provides advice, help, and inspiration, usually to those younger or less experienced

naturalized To have gained citizenship of another country, usually not the one in which one was born

non-refoulement A principle in international law, which means that people cannot be returned to a country where their lives or freedom may be endangered

persecution Being harassed, arrested, threatened, or even killed, particularly on the basis of religion, political opinions, or ethnic, social, and cultural background

professional Someone in an occupation that requires high levels of learning, training, or experience

ratify To approve something, such as the 1951 Refugee Convention, which many countries have approved and added its principles to their national laws

refugee Someone who has been recognized as being in need of protection (asylum) because he or she is a victim of persecution or has a reasonable fear of being persecuted in the future

seasonal According to the seasons, only available during certain times of the year

sector An area or part of a larger thing. For example, hospitality and catering services are one sector in which someone can be employed

social security A social insurance plan that helps people in need, usually paid for by taxes. In the United States, Social Security refers to the system that provides money to people after they retire

traumatic Something that is frightening or unpleasant, which can have a long-term emotional effect

tuberculosis An infectious disease that primarily affects the lungs

unscrupulous Without scruples, without moral or personal standards of what is good and right

vaccinated Having been inoculated (often by injection) against infectious diseases

visa A stamp or document added to a passport allowing the traveler to enter or leave the country that issued the visa

West Germany One of the two nations, along with East Germany, created by the victorious Allied forces following the defeat of Nazi Germany in World War II. The two were reunified as one country in 1990, at the end of the Cold War

xenophobia An irrational fear of foreigners or strangers

IDEAS FOR DISCUSSION

- *Have you ever migrated yourself? What type of migrant were you—tourist, internal migrant, international migrant, refugee? If you have never migrated, would you like to? Where would you like to go?*

- *Are there any migrants living near you? What kind of employment do they have? Do you think they take jobs away from local people, or do they do the jobs local people do not want to do?*

- *One "hot topic" in migration management is what to do about irregular migration. Read the viewpoints on page 28. What do you think about amnesties for irregular migrants? Are they are a good or bad idea? What are their advantages and disadvantages—for migrants and governments?*

- *Most of the countries that host the largest numbers of refugees are not wealthy countries. How could richer countries help them help their refugee populations?*

- *Are there any ways that you, as a young person, can help new migrants to settle in to your community?*

FURTHER INFORMATION

www.everyculture.com/index.html

Learn about numerous cultures of the world through this cultural encyclopedia. Click on "Multicultural America" to see articles on different immigrant groups living in the United States.

www.migrationinformation.org/datahub/

The data section of the Migration Policy Institute in Washington, D.C. Discover thousands of facts about migration.

www.refugeestories.org/

A Web site about refugees living in London. Listen to people's firsthand stories of what it is like to be a refugee living far from home.

www.unhcr.org

The official Web site of the United Nations Refugee Agency. Contains information and statistics on refugees and IDPs (Internally Displaced Persons) in many.

INDEX

INDEX

ABOUT THE AUTHOR

Ceri Oeppen is a doctoral student at the Sussex Centre for Migration Research, which is part of the University of Sussex. Her dissertation is about Afghan refugees who live in the San Francisco Bay Area, California. She has taught Master's Degree courses on migration issues and has co-edited an academic book on Afghanistan. Ceri lives with her husband Geoff and a Springer Spaniel called Layla. She enjoys traveling and has lived in California, India, and Iran.